The ABCs
of Self Love

Melody Godfred

Dedication

This book is dedicated
to every woman
who chooses herself.

WOMAN:
Reclaim yourself.
Shed the weight of uncertainty.
Of responsibility.
Of pain.
Of disappointment.
Of pressure.
Commit to something better.
Choose.
Choose happiness.
Choose love.
Choose power.
Choose fulfillment.
Choose choice.
Choose yourself.

Acknowledgments

Nearly ten years ago, I wrote my first book. Between then and now, I got married, started two businesses, had three kids, and embarked upon my personal self-love journey.

Throughout it all, creating content that empowers others to recognize their power and worth has been my greatest passion. I wouldn't be here without the support of my family, especially my husband, Aaron, and mom, Jackie. I'm grateful to my kids, Violet, Stella and Theodore for inspiring me daily, and to my teams at Fred and Far and Write In Color, especially Kara Brandt, Nicole Kosoff, and Amanda McMullen for helping me bring this book to life.

Introduction

Ever since I started the Fred and Far Self Love Movement, this is the quote I keep coming back to:

> *"So many years of education*
> *yet nobody ever taught us*
> *how to love ourselves*
> *and why it's so important."*
> UNKNOWN

What I wouldn't give to go back and substitute even one semester of chemistry or calculus for a semester of self-love. So much of the work we do as women is to heal the wounds of our childhoods—because loving ourselves is something we simply weren't taught to do. Thankfully, together we are changing that.

Which brings me to this: I'm excited to share the ABCs of Self Love, a blend of inspiration, education and practical application. Because it's never too late to learn how to love yourself. Never.

With all my love,

Melody

Of all the things I've ever learned,
loving myself changed things the most.

Authenticity & Abandon

When you can stand naked
before yourself,
stripped of guilt and shame,
expectations and regrets,
the woman you will see before you
is your authentic self.

Choose her.

A: Authenticity & Abandon

To love yourself, you must first know yourself, which is why **authenticity** is so critical. When we're born, we are the truest version of ourselves. As we grow up, we accumulate a layer of dust: the dust of expectations, of responsibilities, of conformity, of trauma, of pain. This dust dulls our essence, our most authentic selves.

Take a moment to think back to your childhood self. That authentic, dust-free version who made choices from a place of love instead of fear, and instinct instead of learned behaviors. Once you discover that authentic self, imagine abandoning the dust, the stories, the self-imposed limiting behaviors and thoughts that have kept your magical, authentic self hidden.

That person you're envisioning right now? That's your ME. Let's go find her.

SELF-LOVE IN ACTION:

Find a happy picture from your childhood and use it as the home screen image on your phone. When you see it, reconnect with her, your most authentic self. Remember what made her happy before she was covered in the dust of adolescence and adulthood.

As you go through your day, ask yourself:
What would my ME do?

B

Boundaries

Say yes when the answer is yes.
Say no when the answer is no.
Self-love is how you know the
difference between the two.

B: Boundaries

Boundaries aren't just about drawing a line. They are about knowing yourself enough to know where the line should be drawn and having the confidence and self-worth to honor the line. No two people have the same needs. A boundary ensures that both you and the people in your life know what your needs are so you can both honor them.

Not sure if someone has crossed one of your boundaries? Check in with your body. When something happens and in response you feel off, chances are a boundary was crossed.

For boundaries to work, you must engage two qualities: flexibility and vulnerability. Since your needs are constantly evolving, no boundary is ever absolute. You have to consistently check in with yourself and see if the boundary is still accurate. In order for a boundary to exist in the world, you must communicate it, which takes vulnerability. If you're anything like me, confrontation is highly uncomfortable. Communicating a boundary may require a small confrontation, but having a boundary is what alleviates the need for big confrontations down the road.

Setting a boundary can be intimidating, but ultimately it is both exhilarating and freeing. The first time you set one, communicate it, and stick to it, you'll see.

SELF-LOVE IN ACTION:

Practice setting boundaries. For each category, set a boundary and then communicate it: friends, family, love, work, play. Keep in mind: boundaries aren't just about saying no, they are also about saying yes!

Here's an example:

Friends: No therapy sessions for friends before 11 am
Family: No saying yes purely out of obligation
Love: No important conversations via text
Work: No checking work emails after seven
Play: Yes to fun experiences with people I enjoy

Your turn:

Friends:

_____
_____

Family:

_____
_____

Love:

_____
_____

Work:

_____
_____

Play:

_____
_____

Boundaries aren't about what you say no to. They're about what you make space for.

The Four C's:
Clarity, Commitment,
Creation & Community

*Self-love and sisterhood
will save the planet.*

The Cycle of Self

You begin by knowing yourself. Your essence. Your ME. This is self-discovery.

As you discover your needs, you begin to care for them. You make time, you make space. You nurture yourself with your attention and commitment.
This is self-care.

You know who you are, and you embrace yourself. The good, the bad, the light, the dark.
This is self-acceptance.

You own your worth and fuel it.
You are whole without the infusion of anyone else's energy, acceptance, love, care, or praise.
This is self-worth.

And you continue. On and on. Over and over. You commit to this cycle of self- discovery, self-care, self-acceptance, and self-worth.
This is self-love.

C: The Four C's:
Clarity, Commitment,
Creation & Community

When choosing a diamond, there are four C's: cut, clarity, color and carat weight. When it comes to choosing yourself, there are four C's as well that together embody the steps along the cycle of self.

The first C stands for **clarity**, which represents getting to know your authentic self, needs, wants and goals.

The second C stands for **commitment**, which represents committing to daily practices that honor your true self and nurture your mind and body.

The third C is **creation** (magic!), which is what you manifest when you choose yourself daily.

The fourth C is **community**, which is what you should cultivate around you to support your commitment to yourself.

Remember: self-love isn't a destination. It's a continual cycle that is at the heart of all wholeness and human connection.

Wherever you are on your journey, let the four C's guide you.

SELF-LOVE IN ACTION:

For each day this week, pick one of the four C's to focus on.

Monday
Clarity: spend 15 minutes first thing in the morning journaling in response to these prompts:

I am...

_____

_____

I need...

_____

_____

I want...

_____

_____

I believe...

_____

_____

I know...

_____

_____

I can...

_____

_____

I will...

_____

_____

Tuesday

Commitment: devote at least one hour today to self-care. Write down how you felt afterwards:

_____

_____

_____

_____

Wednesday

Creation: enjoy yourself today by doing something that feeds your soul. What did you create?

_____

_____

_____

_____

Thursday

Community: plan a girls night and make vision boards to empower your self-love journeys. Write down what you want your board to focus on:

_____

_____

_____

_____

Friday

Reflect on how you feel today compared to how you felt at the beginning of the week:

_____

_____

_____

_____

_____

_____

*Dreams only come true
if you have them.*

D

Daily Dream

Dreaming big so there's room for all the different women in me.

D: Daily Dream

Chances are you have a To Do list, whether it's written down in a notebook, exists digitally on your phone and computer, or is simply a mental load you struggle to keep up with. The question is, when you review that list, what percentage of it relates to soul-sucking aspects of your day (i.e. paying bills), as opposed to soul-filling ones (i.e. dreaming)?

Until recently, dreaming wasn't on my list. And as a result, my spirit was slowly succumbing to the responsibilities of my everyday life. That's when dreaming came in and changed things. A friend and I set a calendar alert called **DAILY DREAM** for 5 pm every day. When it goes off, we spend 15 minutes dreaming and then we text each other about it. Once we started creating space to dream, our dreams started coming true. Not all of them, and not all at once, but as we became more intentional about dreaming, we were able to transform our lives into lives worth dreaming about.

SELF-LOVE IN ACTION:

Set a calendar alert that repeats called DAILY DREAM. Invite your bestie to dream with you. Text each other your dreams, celebrate each other for dreaming, and celebrate again when your dreams come true.

E

Emotional Empowerment

*All the ways
we try to avoid our pain
when the only way through
is to feel it.*

E: Emotional Empowerment

Two of the phrases we hear most often as babies and children are, "Don't cry" and "You're okay." And so, we're raised to believe that painful feelings shouldn't be expressed or felt. We all know what follows— a lifetime of buried feelings like shame, guilt, pain, anger, frustration and sadness— that isolate and debilitate us. Instead of feeling our "unapproved" feelings and allowing them to show us the root causes of our discomfort, we do everything we can to avoid them. We carry them around like our shadows.

Emotional empowerment is about feeling all of our emotions and inviting them to transform our lives. It is about practicing complete self-acceptance so that no feeling is off limits. Once we feel what needs to be felt, we can decide how we want to think and act next. Think of your feelings as a teacher instead of a burden, and let feeling everything become as natural as breathing. Because once you feel, you can explore, release and move on, and motion is the root of life, growth, and of course, self-love.

SELF-LOVE IN ACTION:

Spend the day feeling your feelings and getting curious about them. As emotions come up, create space for them (instead of burying or judging them), and then ask yourself, "How come?"

Follow the "how comes" until you get to the root issue, and then see if there's anything you can do to change it. If not, see how you can shift your perspective to create peace of mind and acceptance.

Feeling: _____

How Come?

_____

_____

Feeling: _____

How Come?

_____

_____

Feeling: _____

How Come?

_____

_____

Feeling my feelings instead of reacting to yours.

Forgiveness (Freedom)

Forgive.
Not because they deserve it,
but because you do.

F: Forgiveness (Freedom)

Want to feel truly free? **Forgive, forgive, forgive.**

The root of "forgive" comes from the Latin word, "*perdonare,*" which means "to pardon; to give completely, without reservation." This is the kind of forgiveness you owe not just to those who have hurt you, but also to yourself.

What makes forgiveness unique is that it is a gift both to the recipient and to the giver. Until you forgive, you remain stuck in the wrongdoing that harmed you (which only escalates your pain).

Forgiveness is what allows you to unshackle yourself from the past so you can live in the present and dream into the future. While your ego may push you to carry a grudge, remember that your ego isn't your true self. Your ego cares about right and wrong, blame and shame. Your true self craves joy, magic, lightness and peace. To honor your true self, it's important not just to forgive others, but to forgive yourself as well, freely, fully, quickly, completely, and without reservation. Because once you do, you'll free your authentic self to create, to love, to heal, and to live unencumbered by the mistakes of the past.

SELF-LOVE IN ACTION:

Write a letter of forgiveness to someone who has wronged you, and write another one to yourself. Whether you share the letters is secondary. The freedom comes from feeling them.

Forgiveness letter to: ME

_____

_____

_____

_____

_____

_____

_____

_____

_____

_____

_____

_____

_____

_____

_____

_____

_____

_____

_____

_____

Forgiveness letter to: _____

_____
_____
_____
_____
_____
_____
_____
_____
_____
_____
_____
_____
_____
_____
_____
_____
_____
_____
_____
_____
_____
_____
_____
_____
_____
_____

G

Gratitude Over Guilt

Choosing yourself might be the hardest decision you ever make because guilt, shame and fear are powerful gatekeepers.

Do it anyway. You are more powerful than they are.

Much more.

G: Gratitude Over Guilt

Gratitude is a word you hear quite a bit once you start exploring self-love, positivity and mindfulness. While the traditional definition— being thankful— is important, I'm going to challenge you to think of gratitude a little differently. For me, gratitude isn't just about being thankful. It is about being truly present in the moment I'm experiencing, instead of feeling guilty about something outside of my current experience.

Let me explain. If you're a working mother like I am, you spend a lot of time feeling guilty that you're not with your kids, instead of feeling grateful that you're at work (and vice versa). The moment I flipped my internal switch from guilt to gratitude, my happiness increased exponentially. And this doesn't just apply to real-time conflicts. Oftentimes, it's the guilt from the past or guilt about something in the future that takes the joy out of a present experience.

Guilt robs you of the moment you're in. Gratitude reclaims it. When we focus on the moment we're in and practice gratitude instead of guilt, we ground ourselves (and especially our runaway thoughts) in joy. Once we do that, self-love becomes second nature.

SELF-LOVE IN ACTION:

Throughout the day, clock your thoughts and keep a gratitude vs. guilt tally. At the end of the day, see how many times you caught yourself in a moment of guilt, as opposed to a moment of gratitude, and challenge yourself to see those guilty moments through a new, more grateful lens. Continue your tally throughout the week, and see if by the end of five days your gratitude thoughts/feelings outweigh your guilty ones.

THOUGHT TALLY

	GRATITUDE	GUILT
Monday		
Tuesday		
Wednesday		
Thursday		
Friday		
Saturday		
Sunday		

Guilt closed my eyes.
Gratitude opened them.

H

Happy Thoughts

She owned her choices,
her thoughts and her moods,
both high and low.
Her happiness was
hers to cultivate.
She was the cause,
the catalyst.
She was her own.

H: Happy Thoughts

It took me reaching an emotional rock bottom to finally seek the help of a therapist. She taught me the most extraordinary truth: **just like I can choose myself, I can choose my thoughts.**

As someone who naturally assumes the worst, learning that I can bend my thoughts to my will changed my life. Imagine you're a surfer and you're sitting on your board in the middle of the ocean waiting for a wave. You see a huge monster of a wave approaching that is certain to bury you. In that moment, you can choose: do I want to get on this wave, or do I want to wait for the next one? Now, when something happens and I feel a negative reaction coming on, I pause and let that monster wave pass me by. I choose to wait for a *nug* (surfer slang for a good wave) instead. It requires mindfulness and patience, which both require work, but it's worth it.

Let me give you another example: I send my friend a text and she doesn't immediately respond. My old, fearful self would immediately assume, "Oh no. I did something wrong. She's mad at me." Now, when that thought presents itself (because it still does), I choose a happy thought instead. "Oh, she is busy. She'll get back to me later."

And that happy thought is the right one 99.9% of the time.

Regardless of the circumstances you're facing, how you think about them is truly 100% up to you. Choose a positive perspective, choose the happy thoughts, get on the happy wave and enjoy the ride.

SELF-LOVE IN ACTION:

Adopt a happy thought mantra. When negative thoughts dominate your mental ocean, repeat your mantra a few times to slow your mind down, and then try to see the situation you're facing from a different, happier perspective.

Examples:

I choose happiness
Head up, heart open
I deserve joy
The future is bright

If repeating a mantra isn't intuitive for you, choose a happy song instead, like *Happy* by Pharrell, that you can think about or play when you need it.

MY HAPPY THOUGHT MANTRA (OR SONG):

Your job isn't to make
someone else happy.
Your job is to
make yourself happy
and then
surround yourself
with others
doing the same.

I

Intuition & Intention

*Stop thinking and
start knowing.*

I: Intuition & Intention

You know that funny "knowing" feeling you get sometimes, the one deep down in the pit of your stomach or on the edges of your mind? The one that signals something to you without you knowing exactly how or why? Meet your **intuition**. The advocate you didn't know you had.

The beauty of intuition is that it is inherent, not learned, and doesn't need any facts or justification to make its case. She's there for you, watching out for you, all the time. The problem is that in most cases, we're simply too busy, distracted, or skeptical to recognize or hear her. Your intuition is the voice of your true, authentic self, your ME, the part of you that is tapped into the divine feminine and thus the universe. Once you start listening for her, your intuition will be impossible to miss. She'll reach for you through your other senses as well, so pay attention to bodily cues. Once you feel connected to your intuition, the second piece comes: intention.

Use your intuition as guidance to become intentional in how you live your life. Make choices that align with and honor your authentic self. Because once your intentions are aligned with your intuition, your life will transform into one that resonates with you on a mind, body and soul level.

SELF-LOVE IN ACTION:

Create space so your intuition can speak up. Allocate five minutes each morning and five minutes before bed to meditate and free your mind of the clutter that drowns out your intuition.

Find a comfortable spot, sit in a resting position, and let your mind and body slowly relax into a place of being instead of doing. Breathe in for five counts; breathe out for ten.

If you have trouble quieting your mind, use a mantra to center yourself, or engage in a repetitive (non-digital) movement like playing scales on an instrument, weeding your garden, going for a run or taking a shower.

Now listen, not just in your mind but also in your body, for cues and guidance.

Another space where you can listen for your intuition is in your dreams.

Write down the things your intuition shows and tells you in both your waking and dream life. Once you start paying attention, you'll realize she talks to you and helps you all the time.

My ME creates space
for the unknown.
She can remember the past without
being defined by it.
She can manifest the future without
being tied to it.
She is present.
She is peaceful.
She is powerful.

J

Joy

Sometimes
I'm a happy ray of sunshine.
Sometimes I'm a melancholy
beam of moonlight.
Happy or sad, I am still whole.
I am still worthy.
I am still enough.
I am still grateful.
I am still joyful.
I am still ME.

J: Joy

While the terms happiness and **joy** are oftentimes used interchangeably, they are actually two distinct pieces of the self-love equation that work together.

Whereas happiness is a state of mind that comes in response to external experiences, joy is a more constant, internal state of being. For example: happiness is when you start getting paid for your creative work. **Joy** is knowing your art is worthy of an audience regardless. One is externally triggered, the other is deeply connected to your internal sense of worth, peace and wellness. While happiness is important, joy is critical— as only joy will sustain you through whatever highs and lows life presents.

When it comes to self-love, we talk a lot about embracing and experiencing your darkest feelings. But according to Dr. Brené Brown, it takes just as much courage (if not more!) to experience your joy as it does to embrace your sorrow. "Joy is the most vulnerable emotion we experience," Brown says. "And if you cannot tolerate joy, what you do is you start dress rehearsing tragedy." Dress rehearsing tragedy is when you disclaim your joy by preparing yourself for the worst (which is sure to follow... or is it?).

Joy is a state of being that requires nurture in the form of gratitude and trust. It also requires that you get very comfortable with uncertainty because the circumstances both within you and external to you can change. So when you feel the warm glow of joy radiate from within, really feel it and let it carry you through everything that follows.

SELF-LOVE IN ACTION:

Sometimes the joy within us becomes dormant due to the weight of our routines. To wake up your joy, shake up your rituals. Commit to one week of new everything: new shampoo or soap to change the scent in your shower, a new breakfast, a new route to work, new music, a new workout class, a new bar/restaurant/museum for after work. Make plans with a new friend. Take a last minute day trip. Change up your going-to-bed ritual. Shop for a little something new for yourself.

At the end of the week, all the newness should wake up the spark of joy within you. From there, use gratitude to nurture it, and make the new things that worked part of your weekly rituals.

NEWNESS LIST
Write down the new things you tried and loved

_____

_____

_____

_____

_____

_____

_____

_____

_____

_____

_____

_____

_____

_____

_____

_____

_____

_____

_____

_____

_____

_____

K

Know Your Narrative

*You're the only YOU
who'll ever exist.
What a responsibility.
What a gift.*

K: Know Your Narrative

To love yourself, **know and own your narrative**. Your narrative is your story. It is the unique blend of inherent magic and earned experience that makes you uniquely you. It is what allows you to leave an imprint on the world in a way no one else can.

Once we realize the power that comes with being one in nearly eight billion, we can start reclaiming all parts of ourselves and our stories instead of disclaiming them.

What once was a source of shame is now a source of strength. What was once a series of disconnected events and outcomes is now the one-of-a-kind formula that belongs only to you. Instead of seeing yourself as a series of circumstantial events and characteristics, see the through line: the you that connects it all.

Know your narrative and embrace it with pride. Because yours is the story of a lifetime.

SELF-LOVE IN ACTION:

Grab a journal and write one page for every year of your life. Write the year in big block letters at the top of the page, and dive into your mental, emotional and physical memory. Write about what happened and how you felt. Once you're done, see if you can identify some common themes, and start constructing your narrative's through line.

Also, use this as an opportunity to revisit and heal old wounds, and forgive yourself and others for any events that caused you to lose sight of your authentic self, power and magic.

*The power of this movement
isn't that we are the same.
It's that we are each
one of a kind,
and stand for each other
in celebration of that fact.*

Light

Self-love is light.
It illuminates.
It uplifts!

L: Light

The definition of the word "light" is one of my favorites. The word encompasses so many unique definitions, and yet they play into each other so gracefully. Light is what stimulates sight and makes things visible. Light is brilliance. Illumination. To see the light is to become enlightened— to unravel a mystery. A light is the flame. To light is to burn. To be a light is to be a leader, a luminary, an expert. Lightness is simplicity. Ease. Gentleness. Weightlessness. Freedom from worry. Freedom itself.

When practicing self-love, be light. In its myriad of definitions. Be the light that illuminates the world. Shed the weight of uncertainty, risk, anger, resentment, doubt, guilt and shame, and be light. Unravel the mystery of yourself and set your soul on fire. Be light, be light, be light.

SELF-LOVE IN ACTION:

Use the power of a flame as your symbol of self-illumination and empowerment. Light a candle every night for a week, and as you watch the flame, imagine it is your own inner light flickering. Go within yourself and discover what your light needs so you can feel light, give light, be light.

M

Manifest Your Magic

Businesses, babies, homes, art, cultures, civilizations: we create. Oftentimes out of nothing and with the odds stacked against us So when we say women are magic, believe us.

M: Manifest Your Magic

Magic is what happens when your thoughts, actions and feelings are in alignment with your authentic self, your ME. What is your ME? It's the part of you that is and always was. Before the guilt. The trauma. The pain. The doubt. The responsibility. Even when you ignore your ME, she is there. Patient. Hopeful. Resilient. All she wants is your nurture, your love, your attention, your care. And what she'll give you in return for those things is everything. Peace of mind. Wholeness. The energy, passion, creativity, and motivation you've been missing. In a word, magic.

What does it mean to **manifest magic**? It means that you let your ME start leading your life (playing offense) instead of letting life happen to you (playing defense). It means you create the world around you by deliberately choosing your thoughts and actions instead of constantly being in a reactive, negative space where you assume the worst and make sure you're right.

Because you are a creator, whether you've realized it yet or not, your magic is inherent, not earned. Let your ME lead you to it. And once your magic is clear and within grasp, use it to make the contribution to the world that only you can. Because your ME, your magic, and your ability to manifest are all uniquely yours.

SELF-LOVE IN ACTION:

Gather 10 items that embody elements of your most authentic self and use them to conduct a magic ceremony. Light candles, take deep breaths and invite your ME to come out and play by reciting these words:

I welcome my authentic self to come to the surface.
I am ready to let her lead.
I trust her, I love her, I am her.

Here's my MAGIC 10*:

1. A spritz of Jo Malone orange blossom perfume (the scent that embodies the orange tree outside my childhood window where I did most of my dreaming)
2. A cassette tape of the song I recorded at 13 (my most meaningful act of creation during adolescence)
3. A page from my childhood diary (where I explored and captured my deepest feelings)
4. Something red (my favorite color, forever)
5. A copy of anything by Toni Morrison (she embodies my love for reading and writing)
6. A souvenir from Italy (where I learned how much I love to explore culture)
7. A string of beads (because making jewelry has been my thing since childhood)
8. Dark chocolate (the taste of pure pleasure)
9. John Mayer (the music that has carried me through the last two decades)
10. A photograph of my family (my joy and home base)

THE MAGIC TEN

1. _____

2. _____

3. _____

4. _____

5. _____

6. _____

7. _____

8. _____

9. _____

10._____

This list was easy to write because since founding Fred and Far, I've been more in alignment with my authentic self than at any other point in my adult life. I hope creating your list of things will help you reconnect with your true self and open the door to manifesting your magic. The magic I have manifested is being with you, here, now. Thank you.

N

Nurture Your Nature

*I reveal myself to myself
and revel in myself.*

N: Nurture Your Nature

Nature vs. nurture: a question we've been asking since the dawn of time with no definitive answer. That is until now. That's right. I've figured it out. In 2012, I gave birth to twin girls who are polar opposites: Stella Avery and Violet Harper. Stella is a replica of my husband: tall, blonde, naturally positive, at peace with herself and the world. And Violet is my mini-me: petite, brunette, emotionally complex, and extremely responsible. Six years later, they are exactly who they were at birth, completely themselves, and completely the opposite of each other despite having exactly the same environment and upbringing. They are simply becoming more vivid versions of who they were born to be.

So, the social experiment is done. It's nature. That was simple, right? Except it's not just about nature. It's about knowing and **nurturing your nature**, and building a life that honors it, that allows you to thrive to your fullest, inherent potential. And that I suppose is where nurture comes in. As a parent, my job right now is to provide just that, the nurture to their nature. And for me, nurture is about giving them the skills to work with who they already are.

I try to nurture my nature each and every day. I strive to connect with my most authentic self and build a life that honors her. I make sure my environment and experiences are working for me instead of against me.

I strive to achieve an equilibrium that honors all parts of myself.

So if you're unhappy or unsettled in your life, ask yourself: am I nurturing my nature? Are you honoring who you are or fighting her?

Think about who you were as a child before practicality, adulthood, competition, ego, trauma, or other external circumstances got in the way. And then nurture the hell out of your nature until you create a life that lets you be unapologetically you.

SELF-LOVE IN ACTION:

Take a personality test and get to know yourself on a deeper level. Use your findings to evaluate whether the life you've created, from the relationships you prioritize to the work you do, honors your intrinsic nature.

I recommend www.16personalities.com

I am not for everyone.
I am for me.

O

Open Your Heart

Heartopened, not heartbroken.

O: Open Your Heart

Think about this word: heartbroken. You've heard it before. You've seen the emoji. A heart cracked in two. You've felt what this word embodies: pain, brokenness, irreparable harm. Let me introduce you to a new word: heartopened. Now picture the same emoji. A heart cracked in two. But this time, instead of that being a bad thing, imagine it is a good thing. Like Leonard Cohen said, "There is a crack in everything. That's where the light comes in."

The definition of **openhearted** is helpful here. It means to be candid, to be emotionally expressive and responsive. To speak your truth is to be openhearted. To feel your feelings is to be openhearted. To receive emotion from another, you must be openhearted.

A heart opened is a heart that is able to receive. A heart opened is one that has experienced life and survived. To connect with another soul, you need an open heart. To welcome love, light, joy... you need an open heart. To experience the magic of vulnerability, you need an open heart. To create space for possibility, you need an open heart.

So if you're healing from a heartbreak, perhaps all you need is a shift in perspective. Instead of focusing on what happened, focus on what is now possible. Your heart is now open. Embrace the cracks, and let the light flood in.

SELF-LOVE IN ACTION:

Fill the cracks in the heart below with all the things you wish to receive. Love, health, travel, commitment, community, security, intimacy, success, clarity, healing, forgiveness, strength. When you're feeling low, revisit your heart and focus on the possibilities that abound for you and your open heart.

Self-love isn't lust.
It isn't a piercing moment
of unbridled passion.
It's slow and tender.
A steady energetic hum
that fills you up
from skin to soul,
head to heart.
And when you practice it,
it radiates off you,
full of life and light and magic.

P

Progress Over Perfection

*Oftentimes we seek perfection
which is other,
instead of seeking authenticity,
which is ourselves.*

P: Progress Over Perfection

"Practice makes perfect," I was told over and over, week after week. And perhaps back then, during my weekly piano lessons, there was some semblance of truth to that. I practiced and practiced and practiced, and occasionally my fingers would grace the keys in exactly the right sequence at exactly the right pace. I would feel high in my fleeting perfection. Of course, whatever we tell children rarely remains within a singular context. I took that notion of perfection over into all other parts of my life. In school and in my relationships with others and with myself. When it comes to human behavior, perfection is not rare. It is an impossibility. And so I disappointed others and disappointed myself. This only led me further away from my authentic self, which is the closest to perfection any of us ever get.

Now as an adult and as a mother, I've learned the power of words. The words I speak to others, to myself, and especially to my daughters. Even during piano lessons, the lesson is, **"Practice makes progress,"** never perfection. I want the high they feel to come from trying, the journey of experience, rather than from a singular outcome. I want them to infuse their relationships with the same focus on effort, attention, and love, rather than perfection. Because when the focus is on effort rather than outcome, they do better, and they feel better along the way. And so do I. And so will you.

SELF-LOVE IN ACTION:

Words have power, and for most of us, "perfect" is one we use in heavy rotation, especially when it comes to standard, perfunctory responses.

Try eliminating "perfect" from your vocabulary. Think of alternatives that are a more accurate reflection of the sentiment you are trying to communicate for each of the phrases below.

You may find that you have to use a few more words to express your feelings, which in a world where abbreviated text conversations take the place of actual human interactions, might not be such a bad thing.

That's Perfect   _____

Perfectly Imperfect*   _____

Perfect Timing   _____

You're Perfect   _____

In A Perfect World   _____

Yes, even this one counts.

Good things come to those who ~~*wait*~~
practice self-love and self-care.

Question Negativity

*I'm made of trillions of cells.
I'm done letting one negative
thought make all of them suffer.*

Q: Question Negativity

The most precious thing you have is your joy. Hard stop. That's why, when you encounter **negativity** either within yourself or from someone else, you need to stop and **question it.** Because, whereas challenging life events are unavoidable, how you think and feel about them are your choice. The same goes for everyone around you as well.

Let me give you an example. You make dinner plans with a friend. You both arrive at the restaurant on time. The restaurant is running twenty minutes late. Your friend is outraged. "Twenty minutes late? We have a reservation! This is outrageous!" Her blood is boiling. Perhaps now so is yours. Now imagine a different scenario. You again both show up to the restaurant that is running twenty minutes late on your reservation. This time your friend couldn't care less. She smiles at the server, says, "No problem," and then turns to you and asks how you are doing. You spend the twenty minutes chatting, connecting, enjoying each other's company. Were the circumstances different? No. But in scenario one, negativity imbued the facts of the circumstance with darkness. In the second, positivity imbued the facts of the circumstances with light. Where would you rather live, in the light or in the dark?

Choose your company carefully. If you surround yourself with negative people, or people who make you feel negative, negativity will prevail and seep into your soul. Once negativity becomes your status quo, kindness, towards yourself, and towards others, is often its first causality. And without kindness, self-love is impossible.

When you encounter negativity, whether it is in your own mind or in someone else's, ask yourself: is this negativity necessary? Is there another perspective you can embrace? Sometimes the answer will be no. There are circumstances that are so tragic that a negative response is the only one that will suffice. Or maybe even in those circumstances, shifting your focus to gratitude can shield you from the threat that the darkness of negativity poses to your joy. Because even in the darkest of times, there's room for gratitude. Always.

SELF-LOVE IN ACTION:

Evaluate your social media accounts. Unfollow accounts that elicit a negative reaction from you, even if that means disconnecting from friends or family.

Negativity on social media comes in many forms. It can be the celebrity or influencer who makes you feels less than in comparison. It can be the uncle who rages about politics. It can be the long-lost high school classmate who populates your feed with irrelevance.

Unfollowing is one form of setting a boundary. Once you do it, you'll create space for something better.

*I worried myself
into the darkness,
I loved myself into the light.*

R

Rest

Old mentality:

If I'm not working myself to death, I'm wasting my potential.

New mentality:

If I'm not working myself to death, I'm realizing my potential.

R: Rest

In a culture where busyness is prized, **rest** is the ultimate affront. We spend the bulk of our conversations talking about everything we have to do, wearing our tightly packed schedules like a badge of honor. We fill every ounce of empty space with our phones, mindlessly scrolling through Instagram, taking pictures that will get uploaded to a cloud we'll never visit, reading articles that only reinforce our collective obsession with feeling doomed.

Rest is now a four-letter word.

It's uttered with shame when it's uttered at all. "I didn't get anything done today," we lament. And the cycle of busyness continues to spin, churning us up and spitting us out.

It's time to take back the word "rest," and all it embodies. To rest is to create space for your body to heal and your mind to wander. Science tells us that our minds need freedom from constant stimulation in order to thrive. In fact, doing nothing and also thinking about nothing are two of the greatest gifts you can give your body and mind.

It may seem counterintuitive, given our obsession with productivity, but doing nothing is the fastest way to revive yourself and actually get somewhere beyond the hamster wheel of your life. Rest, whether that means sleeping for at least eight hours, spending an afternoon at the beach or in a bath, or simply turning off your phone to take a break from its incessant command over your life is the key to your spiritual, emotional, mental and physical revival. Don't believe me? Give it a rest and see how you feel.

SELF-LOVE IN ACTION:

Schedule in some rest this week. The same way you'd schedule a business meeting, workout class or doctor appointment. Schedule five periods of short rest (two hours or less) and two periods of long rest (five to ten hours). During these periods of rest, avoid technology as much as you can, and let your brain reset from all the digital commotion. Remember: doing less does not make you worth less.

REST SCHEDULE

	START TIME	END TIME
Monday		
Tuesday		
Wednesday		
Thursday		
Friday		
Saturday		
Sunday		

Self-care saved my body.
Self-love saved my soul.

S

Surrender

I thought I knew,
and then I KNEW.
I thought I loved,
and then I LOVED.
I thought I surrendered,
and then I SURRENDERED.
I thought it was over,
and then it BEGAN.

S: Surrender

In war, **surrender** is a bitter, bitter thing. It happens when one side has tried absolutely everything to win and has failed, oftentimes with tragic consequences. And so it's no surprise that when we hear the word "surrender," we resist. We want to be strong. We want to win. We want to stay in control. No matter what.

But just like there are no real winners in war, there is no such thing as complete control.

I used to think that if I was strong enough, I could handle everything on my own (because alone = control). And you know what I realized? Strength based on control is actually quite fragile. Holding all the pieces together is impossible. One wrong move, and everything shatters. Now I aim to be soft. To be fluid, flexible, adaptable, in harmony with my environment and those around me instead of in opposition. If strength used to come from control for me, now it comes from surrender. I've replaced my need for control with grace, trust and curiosity, and see the future as a gift to be received.

Instead of fear for the worst or hope for the best, love yourself in every moment and avoid being attached to a particular outcome. No longer is life about getting to point A or point B. It's about opening the door to a yet unknown point C by being part of the story instead of controlling it.

SELF-LOVE IN ACTION:

When you find yourself highly committed to a specific outcome, ask yourself:

If the thing I want most doesn't happen, then what?

_____

_____

_____

_____

_____

_____

If I stop trying to make it happen, then what?

_____

_____

_____

_____

_____

_____

If I took the energy I'm spending worrying about tomorrow and instead focused on loving myself and my life today, then what?

_____

_____

_____

_____

_____

_____

*I will no longer be
at war with myself.
I surrender.
I win.*

T

Trust

I got you.
You got me.
We got this.

A note to (and from) the Universe

T: Trust

The world is simply a reflection of us. When we **trust** ourselves, we trust the universe. When we don't trust ourselves, we don't trust the universe. And either way, the universe listens and the universe complies.

When you trust yourself, you start building momentum. You make choices. You make moves. You stop waiting, and the universe rewards your faith and conspires in your favor.

When you don't trust yourself and are instead indecisive or self-doubting, the universe is paralyzed. Your doubt invariably makes even the right decisions wrong ones.

Imagine instead if you believed every decision you ever made was the right one. Regardless of the outcome, think about what your world would look like then.

But here's the thing: sometimes, just when you think you have it all figured out, it all falls apart. This isn't the universe testing you. You didn't make a mistake by trusting yourself or trusting the universe. This is just the universe reminding you that progress isn't linear. All is not lost. You're still on your way.

Keep going.

SELF-LOVE IN ACTION:

A daily gratitude practice is one way to cultivate trust. Oftentimes, when good things happen to us, we say, "I can't believe it!" because when you don't trust yourself or the universe, your blessings feel otherworldly. Not real. Not yours. Compare this to how we treat our worries. We believe them. Boy, do we believe them.

To challenge these habits, start or end each day with this gratitude practice:

I believe [followed by all the good things you have going for you]

_____

_____

_____

_____

_____

_____

_____

_____

_____

_____

_____

_____

_____

_____

I don't believe [followed by all the worries or negative feelings you carry around]

_____

_____

_____

_____

_____

_____

_____

_____

_____

_____

_____

_____

_____

_____

_____

_____

_____

_____

_____

_____

_____

_____

_____

_____

U

Union

*All of me
loves all of me.*

Your highs. Your lows.
Your power. Your vulnerability.
Your voice. Your silence.
Your shape. Your light.
Your patience. Your momentum.
Your joy. Your despair.
Your playfulness. Your gravity.
Your hands. Your brain.
Your grace. Your neuroses.
Your forgiveness. Your fire.
Your flaws. Your perfection.
Your desires. Your acceptance.
Your might. Your softness.
Your courage. Your anxiety.
Your mess. Your magnitude.
Your jokes. Your anger.
Your hugs. Your tears.
Your integrity. Your ingenuity.
Your talent. Your conviction.
Your vision. Your resilience.
All of you. That's what I love.

U: Union

Union is a word that is most often used in the context of marriage. It is a word that symbolizes the coming together of two lives in one unbreakable bond.

Self-love is when you choose to enter into union with yourself. It is a serious, lifelong commitment. Just as traditional wedding vows include "in sickness and in health," and "in good times and bad," union requires loving yourself "in sickness and in health" and "in good times and bad." It requires seeing and loving all parts of yourself— mind, body and soul— including your shame, your anxiety, your creativity, your depression, your humor, your genius, your strength, your extra thirty pounds, your guilt, your anger, your mistakes, your triumphs.

When you achieve union, you no longer compartmentalize yourself. You embrace it all. You are you, in all your glory. And that is when you achieve wholeness and take control of your worth.

SELF-LOVE IN ACTION:

Write yourself wedding vows by filling in the blanks:

Dearest _____,

I'm so proud to choose you today. You are without question the most _____, _____ and _____ person I know. We've been through so much together, like when_____

_____

_____.
I've watched with awe as you've risen to every occasion with _____. Your ability to _____ truly sets you apart, and I know that with you the future will be full of _____, _____ and _____.

Thank you for teaching me _____.
For being the embodiment of _____.
For always knowing when I need _____ and giving it to me. For allowing me to be exactly who I am in all moments.

Here are my vows to you: I promise you that I will always _____ and _____. I will never _____ or _____.
As we grow together, I will remember

_____.
And today, tomorrow and always, I will continue to choose you, in good times and bad, in sickness and in health, till death do us part.

V

Vulnerability

I thought becoming an adult would set me free. I now know that children hold the keys to freedom: vulnerability and authenticity.

V: Vulnerability

When did being truthful become difficult for you?

I'm not sure I can pinpoint the exact moment, but I know that it happened somewhere between my childhood and my adolescence. There was a time early on in my life where I was willing to feel anything I needed to feel, say anything I needed to say, be anyone I happened to be. I felt, spoke, and lived my truth.

And then, I started to relinquish my authenticity and vulnerability to conformity. I wanted to be liked, to fit in, to appear strong, smart, talented, maybe even perfect?

It takes a lot of courage to embrace **vulnerability** as an adult after years of hiding from it. It takes a lot of self-love to choose to feel and speak and be authentic and vulnerable when we're surrounded by people living "picture perfect" lives (at least that's what they show us). The thing is: once you drop the mask, the people you should keep in your life will celebrate you and follow suit. Because nothing fuels connection more than realness. And vulnerability is as real as it gets.

SELF-LOVE IN ACTION:

For one week, imagine you're starring in a movie where you have to keep it 100% real all the time. See what happens. I'm banking on a happy ending.

Wholeness & Worth

I'll love myself whole.
You love yourself whole.
And with all our wholeness,
we will love each other.

W: Wholeness & Worth

Once upon a time, we were sold a story. Boy meets girl, they fall in love, they are soulmates reunited, and thus two halves make a whole. And so we learned that in order to feel whole, we need someone to come along and complete us. To love us. To choose us. And with that, we took our worth and wholeness and gave them away.

It's time we write a new story. One where one plus one equals three. Where two **whole** people come together and create something bigger through their commitments to each other, and perhaps more importantly, their commitments to themselves.

Only whole-souled people are capable of rich, lasting relationships because only whole-souled people know that **worth** is not something determined by any external person or circumstance. Just like joy, worth is something that is constant and belongs only to you.

That's why all love is fueled by and predicated on self-love. Until we can love ourselves, how can we love someone else?

SELF-LOVE IN ACTION:

Consider the five most important relationships in your life. Do you engage in them from a place of wholeness and self-worth, or are they predicated on external validation and fulfillment? Can you shift them?

X-Ray Vision

*Healing my wounds
instead of hiding them.*

X: X-Ray Vision

In comic books, superheroes like Superman use their **X-ray vision** to see through solid objects, like walls, to uncover the bad guy hiding behind them.

Imagine if you did the same but used your X-ray vision to discover the core feeling you're experiencing and from there, what is causing it?

According to psychologist Dr. Robert Plutchik, there are eight core feelings: joy, sadness, acceptance, disgust, fear, anger, surprise, and anticipation. Combining these emotions yields 34,000 different outcomes. That's right: as humans we are able to feel 34,000 different ways. The first step towards emotional empowerment is to use your X-ray vision to uncover one of the eight core human emotions. From there, work your way out to understand the nuances of your feelings and heal their causes. You can also use this superpower to understand other people's actions and feelings as well.

Who or what is hiding on the other side of the wall? Use your X-ray vision and find out.

SELF-LOVE IN ACTION:

Search online for Plutchik's "Wheel of Emotion" or Erica Chidi Cohen's "The Feelings Circle." Start putting a name to your emotions, and see how you can trace them to discover their root causes.

Y

You First

Self-care: the radical notion that you deserve your own attention.

Y: You First

Chances are, the first time you heard the phrase self-love, your reaction wasn't positive. That's because we're culturally conditioned as women to think that self-sacrifice is feminine and self-care is selfish.

That. Stops. Here. Right. Now.
It's time to put **you first.**

Loving yourself first doesn't mean loving anyone else less. In fact, when you love and care for yourself, you're able to love others more. One begets the other.

It's time to start thinking about and caring for yourself the way you would your most precious loved one. Because ignoring your needs doesn't make them go away— it makes you, your ME, your most authentic self, go away. And running yourself into the ground only means you have less energy, love and passion to give to the world. Self-care is scientifically proven to be good for your mind and body.

So the next time you feel selfish for loving yourself or taking care of yourself first, remember that by loving yourself, you're engaging in a fierce act of rebellion against years of systematic oppression. And who doesn't want to be a rebel?

SELF-LOVE IN ACTION:

Research says it takes 21 days to create a habit. Use this 21 Day Self-Love Checklist Challenge to make connecting with your needs and putting yourself first instinctual. Do one a day in any order you please (this is all about you honoring you).

- ☐ Cancel something you were doing out of obligation
- ☐ Treat yourself to your favorite meal
- ☐ Revisit a childhood hobby
- ☐ Write down five things that you're grateful for
- ☐ Learn something new to stimulate your brain
- ☐ Tackle a bad habit that stands in your way
- ☐ Stretch for 30 minutes to get in sync with your body
- ☐ Walk in nature to ground yourself
- ☐ Stop multitasking for one day and get focused
- ☐ Do a random act of kindness to feed your soul
- ☐ Set an overdue boundary with someone close to you
- ☐ Give yourself an extra hour of sleep
- ☐ Make some art (doodling counts!)
- ☐ Take 24 hours off social media
- ☐ Cut one toxic person or social account from your life
- ☐ Track how you spend every hour for one day
- ☐ Take a dance class
- ☐ Go to a coffee shop and read a book
- ☐ Splurge on a gift for yourself
- ☐ Take a romantic bath
- ☐ Tell someone something you've been too afraid to share

*If loving myself is wrong,
I don't want to be right.*

Zero Out

*I let go of my expectations and
stopped feeling disappointed.*

*I stopped feeling disappointed and
started feeling alive.*

Z: Zero Out

To **zero out** means to remove completely. And that's exactly what I want you to do with all the painful things you're carrying around instead of addressing.

If it's uncomfortable, say it, feel it, do it, leave it, heal it, and sooner.

Because we are not limitless. We can only hold space for so much. Let's zero out the bad by working through it and releasing it to create more space for the good.

SELF-LOVE IN ACTION:

In accounting, the concept of a zero sum account is when you go through your checking account at the end of the month and allocate every dollar. Nothing is left behind. If any money isn't spent, it gets moved into a savings account. Each month, your checking starts at zero.

Now apply the same strategy to your emotional well-being. Each month, check in with yourself and make sure you can allocate every feeling. Don't let old feelings linger unaddressed. Feel the feelings and zero out your account to achieve emotional freedom.

Afterwards

Congratulations on completing The ABCs of Self Love. I'm so proud of you. You should be, too.

Writing this book wasn't easy, primarily because there is so much that goes into self-love, and there is so much more I could have covered for each letter. B for Bravery. K for Kindness. L for Love.

Now that you have your initial ABCs down, I invite you to explore yourself, and your world, to add more to your self-love vocabulary and practice.

If you need additional resources and support, please visit. www.fredandfar.com and join our community on Instagram @fredandfar.

I do have one favor to ask: if this book supported your self-love journey, I hope you'll leave a review on Amazon. Every review makes it that much easier for another woman to start her self-love education and journey.

Here's the link: bit.ly/theabcsofselflove

With love and gratitude, from my ME to yours,

Melody

I _____,

PINKY PROMISE
To choose myself.
To honor myself.
To remember myself
On a daily basis.

About the Author

Melody Godfred is the founder of Fred and Far: A Self Love Movement. She's passionate about empowering women to choose themselves and transform their lives. She launched the company in 2016 to inspire women to practice self-love and self-care on a daily basis. Today, women in 40+ countries wear her Self Love Pinky Ring™ as a symbol and reminder of their commitment.

She is also the founder of Write In Color, a leading personal branding and career development company. Melody has shared her career advice on Forbes, Inc., and The Muse, and has led multiple corporate trainings. She was a featured mentor at the Teen Vogue Summit and a panelist at the Massachusetts Conference for Women.

Melody lives in Los Angeles with her husband, Aaron, and three children, Violet, Stella and Theodore. This is her second book. Connect with her at melodygodfred.com.

Radical Parting Thoughts:

1. It's okay to feel deeply
2. It's okay to speak freely
3. It's okay to think differently
4. It's okay to live openly
5. It's okay to rest daily
6. It's okay to change frequently
7. It's okay to be yourself,
proudly and lovingly.